The Person of the Holy Spirit

Bisi Oladipupo

Springs of life publishing

Copyright © 2022 by Bisi Oladipupo

Springs of life publishing

ISBN: 978-1-915269-13-3 (ePub e-book)
ISBN: 978-1-915269-14-0 (paperback)

All Rights Reserved.

No part of this book may be used or reproduced by any means, graphic, electronic, or mechanical, including photocopying, recording, taping, or by any information storage retrieval system without the written permission of the publisher except in the case of brief quotations embodied in critical articles and reviews.

Printed in the United Kingdom

Unless otherwise indicated, scripture quotations are taken from the King James Version.

Scripture quotations from The Authorized (King James) Version. Rights in the Authorized Version in the United Kingdom are vested in the Crown. Reproduced by permission of the Crown's patentee, Cambridge University Press.

Scripture quotations marked (AMP) are taken from the Amplified Bible, Copyright © 2015 by The Lockman Foundation. Used by permission.

Contents

Dedication	V
Foreword	VI
1. Introduction	1
2. The Holy Spirit in the Old Testament	3
3. The Holy Spirit in the New Testament	7

    Power
    The Holy Spirit Anoints
    He Brings Things to Our Remembrance
    He Shows Us Things to Come
    He Helps Us Pray
    He Convicts the World of Sin, Righteousness, and Judgment
    He Gives Gifts of The Spirit
    He Bears Witness That We Are God's Children

4. The Holy Spirit in the Life of the Believer   19
    How Can the Believer Receive the Baptism of the Holy Spirit Today?
    You Can Fellowship With the Holy Spirit
    The Holy Spirit Can Be Grieved
    Your Body Is a Temple
    Trust the Witness
    Gifts of the Spirit in Everyday Life
    The Holy Spirit Teaches Us All Things
    Praying in the Spirit Helps Us to Build Up Our Sensitivity.
    Our Lord Jesus Christ told His Disciples to Rely on the Holy Spirit.

5. Conclusion   31

Salvation Prayer   33

About The Author   34

Also By Bisi   35

Dedication

To Jesus Christ, my Lord and Saviour—to Him alone that laid down His life that l might have life eternal. To Him that led captivity captive and gave gifts unto men (Ephesians 4:8). One of those gifts is writing!

Foreword

One thing many believers lack is proper discipleship after making Jesus Christ Lord and Saviour.

Unfortunately, not all our churches offer proper discipleship, so we leave our young Christians to sort themselves out.

I remember several years ago when I was told to contact a lady who had recently just become a believer in Jesus Christ. So, I went to see her as she was on my follow-up list.

She made a statement I will never forget. She said, "If a woman gives birth to a child, will she just leave and abandon her? No direction, no contact?" Can you imagine this coming out of a new believer's mouth? In summary, she complained about why she had not heard from the church.

So, what does this have to do with this book's topic?

The honest truth is that many believers do not know the role of the person of the Holy Spirit in their lives. We do altar calls or minister the baptism of the Holy Spirit to believers. They speak in tongues, and this is about all they know. We do not teach nor introduce them to who the Holy Spirit is.

THE PERSON OF THE HOLY SPIRIT

This book will look at the role of the Holy Spirit in the believer's life.

As Christians, we must know the Holy Spirit as a person and cooperate with Him if we are to reach our destinies and help others along the way.

Enjoy the book!

Chapter One

Introduction

Who is the Holy Spirit?

The Holy Spirit is the Spirit of God and part of the Godhead. In the Bible's Book of the beginning, the Book of Genesis, the second sentence in the Bible speaks about the Holy Spirit.

"*In the beginning God created the heaven and the earth.* ^{2} *And the earth was without form, and void; and darkness was upon the face of the deep.* **And the Spirit of God** *moved upon the face of the waters*" (Genesis 1:1-2).

The Holy Spirit was part of creation in the beginning when man was created:

"*And God said,* **Let us make man in our image**, *after our likeness: and let them have dominion over the fish of the sea, and over the fowl of the air, and over the cattle, and over all the earth, and over every creeping thing that creepeth upon the earth*" (Genesis 1:26).

If you notice from the above scripture, it states, "Let us make man" in our image. This refers to the Godhead. The Godhead is God the Father, The Word (Jesus) (Revelation 19:13), and the Holy Spirit (also referred to as the Spirit of God).

"*For there are three that bear record in heaven, the Father, the Word, and the Holy Ghost: and these three are one*" (1 John 5:7).

So, we can see the Holy Spirit has been from the beginning, and He is a person.

"*Now there were in the church that was at Antioch certain prophets and teachers; as Barnabas, and Simeon that was called Niger, and Lucius of Cyrene, and Manaen, which had been brought up with Herod the tetrarch, and Saul. As they ministered to the Lord, and fasted,* **the Holy Ghost said,** *Separate me Barnabas and Saul for the work whereunto I have called them*" (Acts 13:1-2).

He is also known as the Spirit of truth.

"*Howbeit* **when he, the Spirit of truth**, *is come, he will guide you into all truth: for he shall not speak of himself; but whatsoever he shall hear, that shall he speak: and he will shew you things to come*" (John 16:13).

Chapter Two

The Holy Spirit in the Old Testament

In the Old Testament, we can see the person of the Holy Spirit manifested in some people's lives.

While we speak about the Old Testament, it will be difficult not to look at parallels in the New Testament.

God gave Moses an instruction in the Old Testament to build a tabernacle after the pattern shown to him on the mount (Exodus 25:9). The Lord further told Moses that He had called Bezaleel to help in this work.

"*And the Lord spake unto Moses, saying,* ² *See, I have called by name Bezaleel the son of Uri, the son of Hur, of the tribe of Judah:* ³ ***And I have filled him with the spirit of God, in wisdom, and in understanding, and in knowledge, and***

in all manner of workmanship, *⁴ To devise cunning works, to work in gold, and in silver, and in brass, ⁵ And in cutting of stones, to set them, and in carving of timber, to work in all manner of workmanship*" (Exodus 31:1-5).

Here, Bezaleel's gifts and abilities came from the Holy Spirit. Today, the Holy Spirit still gives gifts and abilities (1 Corinthians 12:4).

We can also see people prophesying in the Old Testament when He came upon them. Balaam is one of many accounts.

"*² And Balaam lifted up his eyes, and he saw Israel abiding in his tents according to their tribes; and **the spirit of God came upon him**. ³ And he took up his parable, and said, Balaam the son of Beor hath said, and the man whose eyes are open hath said: ⁴ He hath said, which heard the words of God, which saw the vision of the Almighty, falling into a trance, but having his eyes open: ⁵ How goodly are thy tents, O Jacob, and thy tabernacles, O Israel!*" (Numbers 24:2-5).

The Holy Spirit still gives the gift of prophecy today (1 Corinthians 12:4 & 10).

The Holy Spirit revealed things to come in the Old Testament. David gave Solomon the pattern of the temple he was to build for God, as revealed to him by the Spirit of God.

"*Then David gave to Solomon his son the pattern of the porch, and of the houses thereof, and of the treasuries thereof, and of the upper chambers thereof, and of the inner parlours thereof, and of the place of the mercy seat, And **the pattern of all that he had by the spirit,** of the courts of the house of the Lord, and of all the chambers round about, of the treasuries of the house of God, and of the treasuries of the dedicated things*" (1

THE PERSON OF THE HOLY SPIRIT

Chronicles 28:11-12).

The Holy Spirit in the New Testament still shows us things to come (John 16:13).

Did you know David wrote psalms by yielding to the Holy Spirit?

"*For David himself said by the Holy Ghost, The Lord said to my Lord, Sit thou on my right hand, till I make thine enemies thy footstool*" (Mark 12:36).

"*The Lord said unto my Lord, Sit thou at my right hand, until I make thine enemies thy footstool*" (Psalms 110:1). We can see the person said this by the Holy Spirit. The Holy Spirit is part of the Godhead, and as children of God, we have been given the person of the Holy Spirit. We will look into this in greater detail in some other chapters.

The Bible tells us that prophecy came from the person of the Holy Spirit.

"*Knowing this first, that no prophecy of the scripture is of any private interpretation. For the prophecy came **not in old time by the will of man**: but holy men of God spake **as they were moved by the Holy Ghost**"* (2 Peter 1:20-21).

So, we can see the functions of the person of the Holy Spirit right from the beginning. He is a person. In the Old Testament, we can see the Holy Spirit do the following:

- Gives gifts
- People prophesied by Him
- He reveals things to come

- Holy men in old times were moved by the Holy Spirit to give prophecy of Scripture.

In the Old Testament, they did not have the person of the Holy Spirit live in them as we believers have today. This major difference explains why people had to go to a Prophet to find out what the Lord was saying in the Old Testament. In the New Testament, we can hear God for ourselves. My sheep hear my voice (John 10:27).

Walking and listening to the Holy Spirit is so vital in our walk as believers, and we will look into this in some other chapters.

Chapter Three

The Holy Spirit in the New Testament

We can see that the Holy Spirit has always existed, as He is part of the Godhead. However, in the New Testament, we are privileged to have a greater expression in our lives, especially as believers.

After Jesus Christ died and went to sit at the Father's right hand (Mark 16:19), Jesus Christ our Lord sent the Holy Spirit to abide with us forever (John 16:7 & John 14:16). In the Old Testament, the Holy Spirit did not abide with them. The old saints experienced the Holy Spirit only for a specific purpose. He did not live with them, though He was always at work in some people's lives.

The grand arrival of the Holy Spirit to the earth is recorded in the Book of Acts.

"The former treatise have I made, O Theophilus, of all that Jesus began both to do and teach, ² Until the day in which he was taken up, after that he through the Holy Ghost had given commandments unto the apostles whom he had chosen: ³ To whom also he shewed himself alive after his passion by many infallible proofs, being seen of them forty days, and speaking of the things pertaining to the kingdom of God: **⁴ And, being assembled together with them, commanded them that they should not depart from Jerusalem, but wait for the promise of the Father, which, saith he, ye have heard of me. ⁵ For John truly baptized with water; but ye shall be baptized with the Holy Ghost not many days hence**" (Acts 1:1-5).

"*And when the **day of Pentecost was fully come**, they were all with one accord in one place. ² And suddenly there came a sound from heaven as of a rushing mighty wind, and it filled all the house where they were sitting. ³ And there appeared unto them cloven tongues like as of fire, and it sat upon each of them. ⁴ And they were all filled with the Holy Ghost, and began to speak with other tongues, as the Spirit gave them utterance*" (Acts 2:1-4).

The Day of Pentecost was when the apostles were baptised with the Holy Spirit.

So, what is the role of the Holy Spirit in the New Testament?

The Holy Spirit brings power (Acts 1:8).

The Holy Spirit anoints (Acts 10:38).

The Holy Spirit testifies of Jesus (John 15:26)

He teaches us all things (John 14:26)

THE PERSON OF THE HOLY SPIRIT

He brings things to our remembrance (John 14:26)

He convicts the world of sin, righteousness, and judgment (John 16:8).

He bears witness that we are God's Children (Romans 8:16).

He guides us into all truth (John 16:13).

He gives directions (Acts 13:2; Acts 15:28).

He will show us things to come (John 16:13).

He helps us pray (Romans 8:26).

He gives gifts of the Spirit (1 Corinthians 12:7-11)

He helps us abound in hope (Romans 15:16).

He reveals the truth to us (Ephesians 3:5; 2 Corinthians 2:10)

He is involved in Salvation (Titus 3:5).

He sheds God's love upon our hearts (Romans 5:5).

Bears record in heaven that Jesus came to earth (1 John 5:7).

Bears witness on earth that Jesus came (1 John 5:8).

Now, let us look at some of these functions briefly:

Power

The first place to look at some of the functions of the Holy Spirit is from Scripture.

In the Book of Acts, the Lord told the disciples that they would receive power after the Holy Spirit comes upon them.

"But ye shall receive power, after that the Holy Ghost is come upon you: and ye shall be witnesses unto me both in Jerusalem, and in all Judaea, and in Samaria, and unto the uttermost part of the earth. ⁹ And when he had spoken these things, while they beheld, he was taken up; and a cloud received him out of their sight" (Acts 1:8-9).

If you notice the above scripture, the Lord tells the disciples that the power will come "after the Holy Ghost has come upon them". And if you continue to read the Scripture, it says they would be witnesses unto the Lord. So, it is safe to say the Holy Spirit enables us to be better witnesses of this gospel.

It is said of the apostles that they preached the gospel with "great power".

"And with great power gave the apostles witness of the resurrection of the Lord Jesus: and great grace was upon them all" (Acts 4:33).

"For our gospel came not unto you in word only, but also in power, and in the Holy Ghost, and in much assurance; as ye know what manner of men we were among you for your sake" (1 Thessalonians 1:5).

"And Stephen, full of faith and power, did great wonders and miracles among the people" (Acts 6:8).

THE PERSON OF THE HOLY SPIRIT

Our Lord Jesus Christ, during His earthly time, had a very powerful ministry. If Jesus Christ, our Lord, while on earth, needed the Holy Spirit, so do we.

"*How God anointed Jesus of Nazareth with the Holy Ghost and with **power**: who went about doing good, and healing all that were oppressed of the devil; for God was with him*" (Acts 10:38).

The Holy Spirit Anoints

We have seen from one of the scriptures quoted above that God anointed Jesus of Nazareth with the Holy Ghost and power (Acts 10:38).

Now, if you notice, the scripture states, "How God anointed Jesus of Nazareth". In other words, Jesus Christ was anointed as a man, a man like us—"Jesus of Nazareth". If Jesus Christ, our Lord, during His earthly ministry, was anointed, we need to be anointed.

Our Lord, Jesus Christ, said this during His earthly ministry:

"*The Spirit of the Lord is upon me, because **he hath anointed me to preach the gospel** to the poor; he hath sent me to heal the brokenhearted, to preach deliverance to the captives, and recovering of sight to the blind, to set at liberty them that are bruised*" (Luke 4:18).

The Lord will anoint us for what He has called us to do.

We all have been anointed, and we must learn to yield to the anointing. The anointing also teaches us.

"But the anointing which ye have received of him abideth in you, and ye need not that any man teach you: but as the same anointing teacheth you of all things, and is truth, and is no lie, and even as it hath taught you, ye shall abide in him" (1 John 2:27).

He Brings Things to Our Remembrance

"But the Comforter, which is the Holy Ghost, whom the Father will send in my name, he shall teach you all things, and bring all things to your remembrance, whatsoever I have said unto you" (John 14:26).

Have you found yourself in the place of prayer, and you suddenly remember an instruction the Lord gave you some time ago that you forgot? That is the Holy Spirit reminding you of what the Lord had instructed you to do.

Or you could be praying, and you suddenly remember someone but forget their name. Just ask the Holy Spirit to bring the person's name to your remembrance, and He will.

We must also know that the Holy Spirit will help us with natural things. Next time you forget where you put your house key, ask the Holy Spirit to remind you of where you left them. We need to learn how to walk with the Holy Spirit. Start with small things. In the place of prayer, if you forget a scripture, ask Him to remind you.

He Shows Us Things to Come

The Holy Spirit shows us things to come. Before Jesus Christ died and rose again, the Holy Spirit came upon men and women of God, even in the New Testament, before Jesus Christ paid the price for us and sent us the Holy Spirit to abide with us.

We can see an example of the Holy Spirit showing people things to come in the New Testament. We can see an account in the Book of Luke when Jesus Christ was presented to God in Jerusalem by His earthly parents.

"*21 And when eight days were accomplished for the circumcising of the child, his name was called Jesus, which was so named of the angel before he was conceived in the womb. 22 And when the days of her purification according to the law of Moses were accomplished, they brought him to Jerusalem, to present him to the Lord; 23 (As it is written in the law of the Lord, Every male that openeth the womb shall be called holy to the Lord;) 24 And to offer a sacrifice according to that which is said in the law of the Lord, A pair of turtledoves, or two young pigeons. 25 And, behold, there was a man in Jerusalem, whose name was **Simeon; and the same man was just and devout, waiting for the consolation of Israel: and the Holy Ghost was upon him.** 26 And it was revealed unto him by the Holy Ghost, that he should not see death, before he had seen the Lord's Christ. 27 And he came by the Spirit into the temple: and when the parents brought in the child Jesus, to do for him after the custom of the law, 28 Then took he him up in his arms, and blessed*

God, and said, ^{29} Lord, now lettest thou thy servant depart in peace, according to thy word: ^{30} For mine eyes have seen thy salvation" (Luke 2:21-30).

We can see from the above that the Holy Spirit told Simeon he would not see death until he saw Jesus Christ our Lord. The Holy Spirit reveals things to come.

I remember an incident where the Holy Spirit revealed to me that a friend of mine would not get admission to where she wanted to attend. I told her, and it happened exactly the way I saw it. Although my friend was not yet a Christian at that time, the incident brought her to the Lord, and she gave her heart to Jesus Christ.

He Helps Us Pray

We have a great privilege that the Holy Spirit helps us pray. This is why every believer should ask and receive the baptism of the Holy Spirit after they make Jesus Christ the Lord of their lives. The Holy Spirit is a gift; we just need to ask (Luke 11:13).

While there is nothing wrong with praying in our natural language, we will be limited. Our minds can only know so much; we need the help of the Holy Spirit to pray beyond what our natural minds know. How would you know to pray for a relative that needs urgent prayer without the help of the Holy Spirit? Let us see what Scripture tells us.

"*^{14} For if I pray in an unknown tongue, my spirit prayeth, but my understanding is unfruitful.*" (1 Corinthians 14:14).

So, when we pray in an unknown tongue, our spirit is praying.

"*²⁶ Likewise the Spirit also helpeth our infirmities: for we know not what we should pray for as we ought: but the Spirit itself maketh intercession for us with groanings which cannot be uttered. ²⁷ And he that searcheth the hearts knoweth what is the mind of the Spirit, because he maketh intercession for the saints according to the will of God*" (Romans 8:26-27).

He Convicts the World of Sin, Righteousness, and Judgment

We share the gospel with others and allow the Holy Spirit to bring the conviction. We give the Holy Spirit something to work with when we share the gospel with others. There is no point in arguing with others; share the good news and leave the rest to the Holy Spirit.

I remember listening to a true account from a gospel minister several years ago. In summary, he said he went to minister somewhere, and he had a strong conviction that he had to have an altar call for people to respond to. This minister also had a word of knowledge.

So, he gave the altar call and the word of knowledge, and he knew who needed to respond, but the person did not respond. He said it was such a strong conviction, and the minister was a guest speaker.

Shortly after the meeting, he received a call from the pastor, who invited him to the church. To summarise, the pastor said he also knew who needed to respond but did not. A few days later, the gentleman in the service who was supposed to respond but did not, got drunk and tried to open someone else's house by mistake. As a result, he was shot and rushed to the hospital. He then called for the pastor to come, and this is what the gentleman said to the pastor, "Why did l not respond to that altar call? l knew that was me; I knew that was me".

It is the Holy Spirit that convicts, but people need to respond.

The mind fights unbelievers in receiving Jesus Christ as Lord and Saviour.

*"³ But if our gospel be hid, it is hid to them that are lost: ⁴ In whom the god of this world hath **blinded the minds of them** which believe not, lest the light of the glorious gospel of Christ, who is the image of God, should shine unto them" (2 Corinthians 4:3-4).*

The Holy Spirit is doing His job, and people need to respond and listen to their hearts.

He Gives Gifts of The Spirit

Have you ever been to a service where the gifts of the Spirit were in operation? Or have you met someone and just received a word of knowledge for them? That is the Holy Spirit at work.

"⁴ Now there are diversities of gifts, but the same Spirit. ⁵ And there are differences of administrations, but the same Lord. ⁶ And there are diversities of operations, but it is the same God which worketh all in all. ⁷ But the manifestation of the

THE PERSON OF THE HOLY SPIRIT

Spirit is given to every man to profit withal. ⁸ For to one is given by the Spirit the word of wisdom; to another the word of knowledge by the same Spirit; ⁹ To another faith by the same Spirit; to another the gifts of healing by the same Spirit; ¹⁰ To another the working of miracles; to another prophecy; to another discerning of spirits; to another divers kinds of tongues; to another the interpretation of tongues: ¹¹ But all these worketh that one and the selfsame Spirit, dividing to every man severally as he will" (1 Corinthians 12:4-11).

We can see from above the working of the person of the Holy Spirit through gifts. Our role is to discern when the Holy Spirit wants to move through His gifts and respond accordingly. Some people have exercised themselves more than others in this area. We all need to desire these spiritual gifts as implored by Scripture (1 Corinthians 14:1).

How would you love it if you talked to someone who did not know the Lord and the Holy Spirit gave you a word of knowledge for the person? It would signify to the person that God is real and indeed interested in them. This is the work of the Holy Spirit.

So, next time you attend any meeting, and the gifts of the Spirit are at work, know it is the Holy Spirit manifesting through His gifts.

He Bears Witness That We Are God's Children

Every child of God will have a witness in their spirits that they are children of God.

"The Spirit itself beareth witness with our spirit, that we are the children of God" (Romans 8:16).

"**16** The Spirit Himself testifies *and* confirms together with our spirit [assuring us] that we [believers] are children of God" (Romans 8:16; AMP).

The role of the Holy Spirit is to bear witness in our spirits that we are children of God. Did you know the Holy Spirit can also bear witness to other things in our spirits? Have you ever had a witness in your Spirit about something? For example, you were about to do something, and you had a witness either to do it or not. Or have you scanned someone in your spirit before?

I remember a time when I met someone, and I was not sure whether the person was a believer in Jesus Christ. I could not ask the person, as he was much older than me. I sensed the Lord say, "See if you can find love". The Scripture says that "God's love has been shed abroad in our hearts by the Holy Spirit" (Romans 5:5). We should be able to discern whether a person is born of God.

These are just a few functions of the person of the Holy Spirit.

Chapter Four

The Holy Spirit in the Life of the Believer

As we have seen, the Holy Spirit has a major role in our lives today. This is one reason we need to acknowledge Him and begin to engage Him in our daily walk with the Lord.

All the functions of the Holy Spirit stated in the previous chapter apply to every believer today. But before we explore more, let us answer a question. How do I receive the baptism of the Holy Spirit today?

The Holy Spirit was sent to stay permanently on earth after Jesus Christ, our Lord, died and rose again (John 16:7; John 14:16-18). This is why our Lord Jesus Christ told the disciples to tarry in Jerusalem until they are endowed with power (Luke 24:25; Acts 1:4). So now, all believers need to do is to ask for the baptism of the Holy Spirit.

We can see the early believers receive the Holy Spirit; they were already believers, yet needed the Holy Spirit's baptism.

"And it came to pass, that, while Apollos was at Corinth, Paul having passed through the upper coasts came to Ephesus: and finding certain disciples, [2] He said unto them, Have ye received the Holy Ghost since ye believed? And they said unto him, We have not so much as heard whether there be any Holy Ghost. [3] And he said unto them, Unto what then were ye baptized? And they said, Unto John's baptism. [4] Then said Paul, John verily baptized with the baptism of repentance, saying unto the people, that they should believe on him which should come after him, that is, on Christ Jesus. [5] When they heard this, they were baptized in the name of the Lord Jesus. [6] And when Paul had laid his hands upon them, the Holy Ghost came on them; and they spake with tongues, and prophesied. [7] And all the men were about twelve" (Acts 19:1-7).

We can see from the above account that they were already believers, yet they had not received the baptism of the Holy Spirit. Another account of believers receiving the Holy Spirit can be found in Acts 8:14-17.

How Can the Believer Receive the Baptism of the Holy Spirit Today?

The same way the early church did by simply asking the Lord, we must not complicate it. The Holy Spirit is a gift, and He is received by simple faith.

A minister of the gospel recounted his experience of asking and receiving the Holy Spirit. This happened many years ago, and at that time, he was young, and the denomination he belonged to taught that a person has to tarry, which means seek and wait for the Holy Spirit. He said he would go to the altar and tarry, wait and cry for years, but nothing happened. Then one day, he read a book on how to receive the Holy Spirit from a general of the faith who is now with the Lord. He said within minutes, he received the Holy Spirit and spoke in tongues. He thought to himself, "Is it this simple? What was all that tarrying about?" He learnt a valuable lesson that sometimes we complicate things.

As a child of God, the Holy Spirit is a gift Jesus Christ promised to send when He left (John 16:7). The Holy Spirit is already on earth now, as Jesus Christ said, and there is no need to tarry. Just ask, and you shall receive.

Now that we have seen how to receive the Holy Spirit as a believer and understand His role in our lives, we will look more into our relationship with Him.

You Can Fellowship With the Holy Spirit

Did you know you can have fellowship with the Holy Spirit?

"*The grace of the Lord Jesus Christ, and the love of God, and the communion of the Holy Ghost, be with you all. Amen*" (2 Corinthians 13:14)

"*The grace of the Lord Jesus Christ and the love of God, and the fellowship of the Holy Spirit be with you all*" (2 Corinthians 13:14; AMP).

We must begin to relate to the Holy Spirit as a person. It takes faith, as we don't see things physically, but these are spiritual realities.

The Holy Spirit Can Be Grieved

We are told not to grieve the Holy Spirit. This means He can be grieved. What does it mean to grieve a person? To upset or make them unhappy about a thing. We can see the Lord was grieved with mankind in the days of Noah when sin multiplied on the earth, and the Lord had to wipe the earth out with water.

"*And it repented the Lord that he had made man on the earth, and it grieved him at his heart*" (Genesis 6:6).

The Holy Spirit also can be grieved, "*And grieve not the holy Spirit of God, whereby ye are sealed unto the day of redemption*" (Ephesians 4:30).

Our responsibility is to obey the Holy Spirit's leadings and act on what He tells us to do. We need to cultivate the act of listening to the Holy Spirit at all times.

Your Body Is a Temple

Did you know your body is the temple of the Holy Spirit? How would you ensure the money is secure if you were given a million dollars to keep in your house? You would put all measures in place to ensure no intruder can get into your house.

Our earthly bodies house the Holy Spirit. It takes meditation to realise the full impact of this.

"*What? know ye not that your body is the temple of the Holy Ghost which is in you, which ye have of God, and ye are not your own? 20 For ye are bought with a price: therefore glorify God in your body, and in your spirit, which are God's*" (1 Corinthians 6:19-20).

So, how do we glorify God in our bodies? By taking care of it.

Trust the Witness

It has been mentioned before that the Holy Spirit bears witness with our spirits that we are children of God (Romans 8:16). He also bears witness to other things. The Holy Spirit is the Spirit of truth, and the wise go with the witness.

Proverbs 14:25 reads, *"A true witness delivereth souls: but a deceitful witness speaketh lies"*.

When we rely on the witness of the Holy Spirit to a situation that appears contrary, it will save us. The Holy Spirit can save us from unnecessary worry and trouble if we learn to listen to Him.

This is a true account.

Some years ago, l was in a church service, and a lady gave a testimony. In summary, she said she was going to travel, and she heard clearly, "Don't board that plane". She said she had heard it at least three times. She knew she was being warned. To cut a long account short, she was waving the ticket on the pulpit. She did not board the plane and guess what happened? The plane crashed with no survivors. Thank God she listened to the warning.

Sometimes, the Holy Spirit gives us burdens to pray for others. We have to obey, as only the Lord knows what needs to be overturned, and He is looking for an intercessor.

I remember an incident when l went out with some friends to a restaurant in central London. We were all seated at the dining table, and l put my bag on the floor beneath the table. After the meal, my bag was nowhere to be found. I did not notice anyone come up to the table during the meal.

THE PERSON OF THE HOLY SPIRIT

I obviously was very concerned; my house key, bank cards, and money were in the bag. However, during it all, l had a strong witness in my heart that the bag would be found intact. To summarise, l eventually got a call from the police station, and my bag was recovered with everything intact. Nothing was missing from the bag—a miracle in central London. All the while, the Holy Spirit was trying to tell me "all is well".

When we learn to listen to the witness of the Holy Spirit, which can be a strong witness or an inner voice, or whichever way the Lord wants to get something over to us, it will deliver us from getting involved in a wrong relationship, unnecessary commitments, and the list goes on.

Mary was told by an angel that she would give birth to Jesus Christ, our Lord. During the visitation by an angel, we have no account that anyone else was there with her (Luke 1:26-38). After this, Mary went to visit Elizabeth, her cousin. Elizabeth is the mother of John the Baptist, and Elizabeth had been barren for a good while (Luke 1:36 & Luke 1:13). Remember, there were no mobile phones in those days. So, when Elizabeth saw Mary, this is what happened:

"*39 And Mary arose in those days, and went into the hill country with haste, into a city of Juda; 40 And entered into the house of Zacharias, and saluted Elisabeth. 41 And it came to pass, that, when Elisabeth heard the salutation of Mary, the babe leaped in her womb; and Elisabeth was filled with the Holy Ghost: 42 And she spake out with a loud voice, and said, Blessed art thou among women, and blessed is the fruit of thy womb. 43 And whence is this to me, that the mother of my Lord should come to me? 44 For, lo, as soon as the voice of thy salutation sounded in mine ears, the babe leaped in my womb for joy. 45 And blessed is she that believed: for there shall be a performance of those things which were told her from the Lord"* (Luke 1:39-45).

We can see that Elizabeth confirmed by the Holy Spirit what the angel had told Mary about her giving birth to Jesus Christ. Now, look at verse forty-five of the above passage again, *"And blessed is she that believed: for there shall be a performance of those things which were told her from the Lord"* (Luke 1:45).

The Holy Spirit, through Elizabeth, bore witness to what the angel told Mary.

We can also see an incident where the Holy Spirit warned the disciples not to go to a certain place.

Now when they had gone throughout Phrygia and the region of Galatia, and were forbidden of the Holy Ghost to preach the word in Asia" (Acts 16:6).

Gifts of the Spirit in Everyday Life

We have mentioned earlier that the Holy Spirit gives gifts (1 Corinthians 12:7-11). These gifts are not just for our church services. As a matter of fact, we have been told to desire spiritual gifts (1 Corinthians 14:1). Spiritual gifts are a tremendous evangelical tool. We can see an example of this during the earthly ministry of our Lord Jesus Christ.

Our Lord Jesus Christ was tired and sat at a well. He then asked a woman to give Him water to drink. During the dialogue, our

THE PERSON OF THE HOLY SPIRIT

Lord Jesus Christ told her to go and call her husband. She replied that she did not have a husband, and the Lord told her how many husbands she had had. Subsequently, the woman went to town to tell everyone about Jesus, and many believed in Him.

"*⁶ Now Jacob's well was there. Jesus therefore, being wearied with his journey, sat thus on the well: and it was about the sixth hour. ⁷ There cometh a woman of Samaria to draw water: Jesus saith unto her, Give me to drink. ⁸ (For his disciples were gone away unto the city to buy meat.) ⁹ Then saith the woman of Samaria unto him, How is it that thou, being a Jew, askest drink of me, which am a woman of Samaria? for the Jews have no dealings with the Samaritans. ¹⁰ Jesus answered and said unto her, If thou knewest the gift of God, and who it is that saith to thee, Give me to drink; thou wouldest have asked of him, and he would have given thee living water. ¹¹ The woman saith unto him, Sir, thou hast nothing to draw with, and the well is deep: from whence then hast thou that living water? ¹² Art thou greater than our father Jacob, which gave us the well, and drank thereof himself, and his children, and his cattle? ¹³ Jesus answered and said unto her, Whosoever drinketh of this water shall thirst again: ¹⁴ But whosoever drinketh of the water that I shall give him shall never thirst; but the water that I shall give him shall be in him a well of water springing up into everlasting life. ¹⁵ The woman saith unto him, Sir, give me this water, that I thirst not, neither come hither to draw. ¹⁶ **Jesus saith unto her, Go, call thy husband, and come hither. ¹⁷ The woman answered and said, I have no husband. Jesus said unto her, Thou hast well said, I have no husband: ¹⁸ For thou hast had five husbands; and he whom thou now hast is not thy hus-***

band: in that saidst thou truly. *19 The woman saith unto him, Sir, I perceive that thou art a prophet* (John 14:6-19).

"*28 The woman then left her waterpot, and went her way into the city, and saith to the men,* *29* ***Come, see a man, which told me all things that ever I did: is not this the Christ?*** *39 And many of the Samaritans of that city believed on him for the saying of the woman, which testified, He told me all that ever I did. 40 So when the Samaritans were come unto him, they besought him that he would tarry with them: and he abode there two days. 41 And many more believed because of his own word; 42 And said unto the woman, Now we believe, not because of thy saying: for we have heard him ourselves, and know that this is indeed the Christ, the Saviour of the world*" (John 4:28-29; 39-41).

So, what triggered this response from the woman? The word of knowledge our Lord Jesus Christ gave caused her to respond in such a way that it won more people to the Lord.

The Holy Spirit Teaches Us All Things

Have you ever found yourself reading your Bible, and suddenly, you got a revelation from a passage you had read for years? Or you suddenly notice something in the scriptures you had not picked up before? That is the work of the Holy Spirit in our lives.

"*But the anointing which ye have received of him abideth in you, and ye need not that any man teach you: but as the same anointing teacheth you of all things, and is truth, and is no lie, and even as it hath taught you, ye shall abide in him*" (1 John 2:27).

The anointing we have received of Him teaches us God's Word and brings us revelational knowledge.

Some people have said that this scripture means you don't need a teacher. This is not what this scripture says. If there were no need for teachers, the Lord would not have teachers as part of the fivefold ministry (Ephesians 4:11).

To fully understand this scripture, we need to look at it in its proper setting.

"*26 These things have I written unto you concerning them that seduce you. 27 But the anointing which ye have received of him abideth in you, and ye need not that any man teach you: but as the same anointing teacheth you of all things, and is truth, and is no lie, and even as it hath taught you, ye shall abide in him*" (1 John 2:26-27).

If you look at the scripture in its setting, it says there is no need for anyone to seduce you. In other words, you don't need to be deceived; the anointing within you will teach you all things.

We need to learn how to listen to our spirits, as this is so important. Sometimes, you might not be able to put your hand on it, but deep down in your spirit, you know that something is not right.

Praying in the Spirit Helps Us to Build Up Our Sensitivity.

"But ye, beloved, building up yourselves on your most holy faith, praying in the Holy Ghost" (Jude 1:20).

Our Lord Jesus Christ told His Disciples to Rely on the Holy Spirit.

"But when they shall lead you, and deliver you up, take no thought beforehand what ye shall speak, neither do ye premeditate: but whatsoever shall be given you in that hour, that speak ye: for it is not ye that speak, but the Holy Ghost" (Mark 13:11).

Chapter Five

Conclusion

The Holy Spirit is part of the Godhead, and He is with us on earth today.

We have seen and learnt about the roles of the Holy Spirit on earth, including His role in the life of believers. This is a spiritual reality, and it takes spiritual understanding for us to engage and apply this great privilege we have in our daily lives. The Holy Spirit is with us and lives in us (John 14:17).

Just think about it. The person who was with God in the beginning is with and in you now! The Holy Spirit that breathed upon the ancient men of God to write our scriptures is the same person with you now. That needs to dawn on us.

We can only walk in what we acknowledge.

"*6 That the communication of thy faith may become effectual by the acknowledging of every good thing which is in you in Christ Jesus*" (Philemon 1:6).

Jesus Christ promised to send us the Holy Spirit when He ascended to the Father, and He has. As a result, the Holy Spirit is now available to every believer in Christ.

I encourage you to pursue your understanding and role of the person of the Holy Spirit and begin to engage Him in your everyday life.

Salvation Prayer

Father God, I come to you in Jesus' name. I admit that I am a sinner, and I now receive the sacrifice that Jesus Christ paid for me.

I confess with my mouth the Lord Jesus, and I believe in my heart that God raised Him from the dead.

I now declare that Jesus Christ is my Lord and Saviour.

Thank you, Father, for saving me in Jesus' name.

I am now your child. Amen.

bisiwriter@outlook.com. Start reading your Bible and ask the Lord to guide you to a good church.

About The Author

Bisi Oladipupo has been a Christian for many years and lives in the United Kingdom with her family.

Bisi attended a few Bible colleges and obtained a Biblical Studies diploma from a UK Bible college.

She is a teacher of God's Word, coordinates Bible studies, and has a YouTube channel at
https://www.youtube.com/c/BisiOladipupo123
.

She writes regularly, and her website is www.inspiredwords-.org
.

Her author page is
www.bisiwriter.com

You can contact Bisi by email at bisiwriter@outlook.com.

Also By Bisi

The Twelve Apostles of Jesus Christ: Lessons We Can Learn

The Lord's Cup in Communion: The Significance of taking the Lord's Supper

Different Ways to Receive Healing from Scripture and Walk in Health

Believing on The Name of Jesus Christ: What Every Believer Needs to Know

The Mind and your Christian Walk: The Impact of the Mind on Our Christian walk

Relationship Skills in the Bible: Scriptural Principles of relating to others

The Nature of God's Kingdom: The Characteristics of the Kingdom of God

www.ingramcontent.com/pod-product-compliance
Lightning Source LLC
Chambersburg PA
CBHW021200080526
44588CB00008B/431